The Nutcracker

The Nutcracker

Barbara Newman

BARRON'S

Woodbury, N.Y. • London • Toronto • Sydney

Also in this series:
SWAN LAKE
PETRUSHKA
GISELLE

First published in Great Britain 1985
by Aurum Press Ltd.

First U.S. Edition 1985 by Barron's Educational Series,
Inc.

This book has been
produced by Aurum Press
Ltd., 33 Museum Street,
London WC1A 1LD.

Edited and illustrated by
E.T. Archive Ltd, 15 Lots Road, London SW10 0QH.

Designed by Julian Holland

All inquiries should be addressed to:
Barron's Educational Series, Inc.
113 Crossways Park Drive
Woodbury, New York 11797

Library of Congress Catalog Card No 85-15021
International Standard Book No. 0-8120-5672-8

Printed in Belgium
567   9 8 7 6 5 4 3 2 1

Front cover: Julie Rose and Simon Rice as Clara and Fritz
with the nutcracker, Royal Ballet, 1984 (Reg Wilson)
Back cover: Model of the nutcracker by Paul Minter from
the design by Julia Trevelyan Oman for the Royal
Ballet, 1984 (Eileen Tweedy)
Endpapers: Design for Act I, the Kingdom of Sweets by
Alexandre Benois (London Festival Ballet)
Title-page: Rudolf Nureyev as Herr Drosselmeyer, Royal Ballet, 1968
(Reg Wilson)

Contents

Barbara Newman is author of three ballet books: *Striking a
Balance, Swan Lake: Sadler's Wells Royal Ballet*, and
You Can Be a Ballet Dancer. In her native New York
she wrote for *Dance Magazine*. Now living in London, she reports
on dance for *The Dancing Times*.

The Plot

Act I
Scene 1

A merry overture begins the ballet, filling the air with a twinkling crispness and a lilt of mysterious exhilaration. When the curtain rises, the scene is set in the snug, comfortable sitting room of Dr Stahlbaum, a government official in a provincial German town; the time is Christmas eve, early in the nineteenth century, and the Stahlbaums are giving a party for their friends and the little playmates of their two children, Clara and Fritz. In the center of the room stands a brightly decorated Christmas tree, glimmering with burning candles and laden with tiny presents; more gifts, too large and heavy to hang on the branches, lie in shiny stacks beneath the boughs. The elegant guests greet one another warmly as they join their hosts in putting the final touches to the decorations, and before long the party is in full swing. As spirited games develop among the children and their parents dance sedately, Herr Drosselmeyer arrives. He is a white-haired old gentleman who wears old-fashioned clothes and a strange black patch over one eye, but he has a kindly nature and Clara and Fritz rush to greet him and to examine the special gifts he has brought with him.

Having silenced the clamoring children and gained the rapt attention of young and old alike, just like a magician, Drosselmeyer produces a series of mechanical dolls in richly spangled costumes and sets them dancing. Delighted by their antics, Clara and Fritz naturally want to play with the amazing dolls, but, despite their eager pleas and sadly disappointed faces, the fragile creations are quickly whisked away before they can be broken. To cheer up the children, Drosselmeyer produces yet another wonderful toy, a wooden nutcracker. He pops a nut between its stiff, painted jaws and brings them together sharply, and the *crack* of the broken shell provides the children with a perfect demonstration of the toy's unique talent. Clara loves the rough-hewn little manikin at once, even though it is far less splendid than the mechanical dolls, and her eyes shine with happiness when Drosselmeyer gently places it in her hands. Fritz, on the other hand, is far from happy; in a moment of jealous spite, he grabs the nutcracker from Clara and runs away with it. As he waves it gleefully over his head, out of her frantic reach, it flies out of his fingers, crashes to the floor and breaks.

Clara gathers up the broken figure and puts it tenderly to sleep in her doll's bed, and her girl friends gather round her to console her. Just to tease the girls, Fritz and his friends concoct a wild game, stamping and strutting among them noisily. Finally the din becomes so great and the children so

Proposed design for the Christmas tree in Act I by Mstislav Doboujinsky for the Vic-Wells Ballet, 1937

flushed and excited that the Stahlbaums call for a stately *Grossvater* dance, grandfather dance, that traditionally signals an end to the festivities. Having thanked their hosts and bundled up their exhausted children, the guests depart quickly. The Stahlbaums send Clara and Fritz straight to bed, lower the lights and go off to bed themselves.

For a few moments, nothing can be seen in the darkened sitting room but the glow of the Christmas tree lights. Then Clara appears in her pale nightgown; although scared by the black shadows and shapes in the familiar room, she has nevertheless returned to give her injured nutcracker one last kiss and make sure he is safely tucked in. A strange whispery sound startles her; just as she spies several mice skittering across the floor, the clock in the corner strikes twelve with deep, ominous notes. Too frightened now to run away or even to move, she crouches down in terror as the Christmas tree grows into a looming tower of lights and the entire room fills with scurrying mice. When the mice fall into menacing ranks behind their King, platoons of toy soldiers march smartly away from the base of the Christmas tree, shouldering their muskets and preparing to rebuff the mouse attack. The nutcracker leaps from his bed to lead the soldiers into the fray, and before Clara's terrified gaze, the two armies clash in a fierce battle. After several charges, Clara herself joins the fight; to aid her beloved nutcracker, she takes off one of her bedroom slippers and hurls it at the Mouse King with all her might. He is destroyed, and in the same instant, the nutcracker is magically transformed into a handsome prince. Bowing graciously to Clara, he invites her to visit the Kingdom of Sweets with him; without a moment's hesitation, she agrees to follow him to that enchanted land.

Above
Herr Drosselmeyer drawn by Bertall in 1847 for the abridged version of Hoffman's tale by Alexandre Dumas

Right
The mice scurrying across the floor, in an illustration by Bertall

Act I
Scene 2

Below
Mary (Clara) and the Nutcracker cross a river on their journey, drawn by Bertall

The Stahlbaum house has disappeared. In its place stands a dense, glistening forest of fir trees, all heavily cloaked in fresh, white snow and glazed with a shimmer of ice. Frosty winds whisper through the branches, blowing up tiny drifts of snow, then a few flurries, and finally a great whirl of constantly shifting snowflakes that swirl and dart at breathtaking speed.

Act II

The Kingdom of Sweets is a fairyland of dazzling spun-sugar palaces, transparent toffee pavilions and gardens of candied flowers that glitter like jewels. When Clara and the Nutcracker Prince arrive, they are welcomed by the dainty Sugar Plum Fairy, who asks them to recount their adventures. After the Prince explains how bravely Clara fought in the battle with the mice, the Sugar Plum Fairy escorts her to a tiny throne and summons many colorful sweets to entertain Clara with their dancing.

First Chocolate performs a sharp Spanish bolero and then Coffee offers a sinuous, slithery Arabian dance and piquant Tea displays its Oriental temperament. A rush of Russians bounce and bound in a lusty Trepak, only to be replaced by a delicate cluster of reed pipes, whose dance bubbles mischievously. Mother Ginger bustles on, herding her ebullient children ahead of her, and then the stage blooms with waltzing flowers. To crown the performance, the Sugar Plum Fairy reappears to dance an elegant duet with her noble cavalier and a delicate, crystalline solo of her own. Finally, all the sweets return to surround the Sugar Plum in one last, magnificent waltz, and the curtain falls on the happiest scene imaginable.

The Libretto

Stories about enchanted nutcrackers are as old as legend, and several versions of them appear in the folk-tales of Bohemia and Poland. But the story of *The Nutcracker* can be traced with accuracy to Germany and to the great story-teller Ernst Theodor Amadeus Hoffmann who in 1816 wrote a tale called *Nussknacker und Mausekönig* (*Nutcracker and Mouse King*) for a volume of stories for children.

Like so many of Hoffmann's masterful creations, this one wove its spell out of an enthralling blend of realism and fantasy. On the one hand, Hoffmann invented Mary and Fritz Stahlbaum, their cosy home in Nuremberg, and the ordinary domestic details of their lives one Christmas eve, an instantly recognizable mixture of wonderful surprises, exasperated parents and broken toys. On the other hand, a series of extraordinary events offset these familiar scenes: tin soldiers jump out of their boxes and shoot sugar plums at ferocious mice, a strong young man stumbles at his task and becomes an ugly doll—and then becomes a young man

Illustration from a German edition of E. T. A. Hoffmann's tale, Nussknacker und Mausekönig

again, and Mary steps into the fur-lined sleeve of her father's travelling coat, mounts a cedar staircase, and emerges in a sunny, magical kingdom.

In Hoffmann's original story, while Mary lies recovering from her fright after the dreadful battle between the mice and the soldiers, Drosselmeyer tells her a story about the beautiful baby, Princess Pirlipat, the wicked Lady Mouseykins who threatens Pirlipat's life, and the search for a brave young man who has never shaved and never worn boots and who will break the shell of the nut Crackatuck in his teeth and save Pirlipat by feeding it to her. In her final cruel attack before she dies, Lady Mouseykins turns the brave young man into a nutcracker—*her* nutcracker Mary quickly realizes—and Hoffmann neatly ends his tale-within-a-tale by returning the action to Mary, whose plucky efforts to help her poor bewitched nutcracker eventually restore him to his human form. He kneels to her in gratitude and rewards her with the journey to the Kingdom of Sweets.

None of this interior tale appears in the ballet. When Alexandre Dumas *père* published his freely adapted translation of Hoffmann's story in 1844, much of the story's mysterious, almost macabre quality, which Hoffmann knew so delighted small children, vanished as well. On

An enchanted Nutcracker in an English children's story, The Wondrous Tale of King Nutcracker and Poor Richard

stage today the darker aspects of the fantasy surface only occasionally. Drosselmeyer is usually portrayed as more eccentric than eerie, and the Mouse King, once a true villain with seven heads and jaws foaming with blood, has dwindled in most instances to mere pomposity.

More than forty years after its publication, Dumas' shorter and much sweeter version of the story was chosen as the basis for a new ballet by the director of the Imperial Theatres in St Petersburg. Ivan Vsevolojsky (1835–1909) was a former diplomat of considerable education, a costume designer with more than 1000 sketches to his credit, and a gifted administrator, whose modifications of the Maryinsky (now Kirov) Theatre's policies persisted long after his tenure (1881–1899). To promote artistic collaboration and a homogeneous style in each new ballet, he created the so-called 'production council', comprising the author of the scenario, choreographer, composer, designer of settings and stage manager. He refused to order settings for a single work from three or four different designers and, breaking with tradition in another area, dissolved the official post of ballet composer to the Imperial Theatres, then held by Minkus, and determinedly sought better composers, like Delibes, elsewhere. Like many noblemen of the time, Vsevolojsky was a confirmed francophile, with a taste more for external elegance in art than profound content, and he considered it his duty and privilege to keep the Tsar's court well entertained.

Above
Alexandre Dumas (1802–1870)

When he conceived the idea of basing a ballet on Perrault's fairy-tale *La Belle au Bois Dormant*, he quite naturally asked the Maryinsky's leading choreographer, Marius Petipa, to translate his conception into movement. He also contacted Tchaikovsky to secure his participation in the new project, even though the reviews for that composer's previous ballet—the first production of *Swan Lake*, which opened in 1877 with choreography by Julius Reisinger—had dismissed the music as 'rather monotonous, dull . . . interesting probably only to musicians'. Having won a commitment from Tchaikovsky, Vsevolojsky worked out a libretto with Petipa and began designing costumes, which he based on Gustave Doré's illustrations for the Perrault tale. In 1890 *The Sleeping Beauty* emerged as the spectacular result of their three-way partnership.

Above
E. T. A. Hoffman (1776–1822)

The Sleeping Beauty proved considerably less successful then with the public than it has since become, but Vsevolojsky believed in it and scheduled it on twenty-one of the forty-five ballet evenings in the 1890/91 Maryinsky season. Eager to maintain Tchaikovsky's involvement in

In Russian the ballet is called Shchelkunchik. *These scenes appeared in the* Annals of the Imperial Russian Theatres, *1892*

ballet and his collaboration with Petipa, he cast about for another fairy-tale ballet subject and hit upon Hoffmann's *Nussknacker und Mausekönig*, a copy of which he had received as a gift in a new Russian translation in 1882. He commissioned music for the new ballet from Tchaikovsky as part of a package deal that also included a one-act opera, and notified Petipa of his choice, instructing the choreographer to base his scenario on Dumas' adaptation.

Petipa struggled dutifully with Dumas' *L'Histoire d'un Casse-Noisette* but could not draw much dramatic or choreographic inspiration from it. In fact, the first draft of his libretto concluded at what we would consider only the mid-point of the ballet, with Clara wandering in a dream into a vast, snow-covered forest. When Vsevolojsky rejected this draft, demanding changes, Petipa read Dumas yet again and eventually seized on the idea of ending the ballet with a set of *divertissements* in the Kingdom of

Sweets, which seems to have satisfied everyone. Certainly Petipa himself was pleased; in the margin of one copy of the manuscript for Act II he wrote, 'This is what I sent to Mons. Tchaikovsky in Paris on March 9th, 1891. I have conquered all difficulties.' Vsevolojsky may also have been delighted since Petipa's Act II now bore a striking resemblance to the latest rage in Paris, the *féerie*, a showy series of *divertissements* meant to be as dissimilar as possible.

Petipa's libretto was a model of precision, a fine-lined blueprint that he, the composer and the ballet's various designers could follow to their mutual benefit. Dividing the action into numbered sections even shorter than scenes, it described not only what happens in each section and to what sort of music but also the approximate duration of the section, measuring time in the number of musical bars required. For instance, in Act I after the children watch the mechanical dolls dancing, Petipa wrote:

12. Clara and Fritz are now overjoyed, they thank Drosselmeyer and go to fetch the toys.
     (*16 bars of a happy, graceful andantino.*)
     The parents forbid them to play with such beautiful things.
     (*The andantino becomes more serious. 8 bars.*)

Or again, at the very end of Act I:

28. Snow begins to fall. Suddenly a snow-storm occurs. Light white snowflakes blow about (60 dancers).
     (*They circle everlastingly to a 3/4 waltz.*)

With this libretto, Petipa set his mark irrevocably on *The Nutcracker*. It is *his* characterization of Drosselmeyer that survives, as he requested music that was 'serious, somewhat frightening, then comic'; *his* selection of *divertissements* that we see, chosen from all the richness of a fabulously specific original text; *his* decision about the Nutcracker's transformation that informs most productions: after Clara throws her shoe at the Mouse King and faints, Petipa simply wrote:

27. The Nutcracker turns into a handsome Prince (*1 or 2 chords*).

Regardless of the many changes that time and various choreographers have imposed on the ballet, its essential structure and development belong to Petipa. As it happened, he did not ultimately choreograph the work himself, but his libretto guided the man who did and laid the groundwork for Tchaikovsky's contribution to this ballet.

The Toy Soldier, one of the mechanical dolls. Atlanta Ballet

The Music

Many believe that *The Nutcracker* would have disappeared from the stage years ago were it not for Tchaikovsky's enchanting music and, indeed, his lyrical scores for *Swan Lake*, *The Sleeping Beauty* and *The Nutcracker* are perhaps the most popular and rewarding in the entire ballet repertory.

Today we take Tchaikovsky's genius for granted, but when he decided to become a musician, his piano teacher, the respected Rudolf Kündinger, tried hard to dissuade him. Kündinger wrote long afterwards, 'At no time did the idea occur to me that Tchaikovsky had in him the stuff of a musician . . . Certainly he was gifted, he had a good ear and memory, an excellent touch, but apart from that there was nothing, absolutely nothing, that suggested a composer, even a fine performer . . . Nothing remarkable, nothing phenomenal.'

Fortunately, Tchaikovsky ignored his teacher's well-intentioned advice. He left his job as a clerk in the Ministry of Justice and in 1862 enrolled in the first class of the newly founded St Petersburg Conservatory. Four years later, having finished his studies, he was invited to teach harmony at the new Moscow Conservatory; he accepted the position and kept it for twelve years, during which time he started, tentatively, to compose.

Tchaikovsky was intrigued by the idea of dance as a stimulus to music long before the directors of the Moscow Theatre commissioned *Swan Lake* from him in 1875. By then he had built a substantial reputation on the strength of his first operas and symphonies, yet he told Rimsky-Korsakov that 'I accepted the work, partly because I want the money, but also because I have long had the wish to try my hand at this kind of music'.

The *Swan Lake* score was brilliantly designed to support and enhance the dance-drama that it accompanied. Drawing his inspiration from what he termed the 'lyrical idea', Tchaikovsky provided haunting musical subjects, very nearly leitmotivs, for individual characters and situations, and flowing rhythmic melodies—ideal for choreographic setpieces—for the *divertissements*. Yet the overall endeavor was not well received, and a discouraged Tchaikovsky left the ballet for more than ten years.

When he returned to compose *The Sleeping Beauty*, his enthusiasm for the venture could scarcely be contained. Upon receiving a copy of the proposed synopsis, he wrote to Vsevolojsky, 'I want to tell you at once that it's impossible to describe how charmed and captivated I am. It suits me perfectly and I couldn't want anything better than

Peter Ilyich Tchaikovsky (1840–1893) photographed in later life by E. Bieber

to write music for it.' Petipa's scenario also pleased him. Far from resenting its meticulous instructions, Tchaikovsky welcomed them—he had, in fact, requested them, hoping to avoid the artistic dissent that had so plagued *Swan Lake*. He sketched out the entire score in about forty days and then began on the orchestration, writing to a confidante, with great insight, 'It seems to me . . . that the music of this ballet will be one of my best creations. The subject is so poetic, so grateful for music.'

The *Sleeping Beauty* opened in January 1890, and again Tchaikovsky's work received only a lukewarm reception. By the time he began composing *The Nutcracker* in March 1891, he was fifty years old. He wrote to his brother, 'I am very tired and suffer a great deal. My uncertainty as to the future weighs upon me . . . My brain is empty; I have not the least pleasure in working.' Although he had enjoyed reading Hoffmann's *Nussknacker* some years earlier, he did not consider it suitable ballet material, and complained to his brother of 'the absolute impossibility of depicting the Sugar Plum Fairy in music'.

Two factors lifted his spirits and spurred his imagination. The inimitable sound of children's instruments which had so attracted him in Haydn's Toy Symphony could, he knew, add immeasurably to *The Nutcracker*. He purchased a whole assortment of them in Paris, and eventually included the trumpet, drum, rattle, cuckoo, quail, cymbals and miniature drums in his score.

He solved a more crucial musical problem with a brand new instrument, 'something between a small piano and a Glockenspiel, with a divinely musical tone . . . [It] is called the Celesta Mustel', he wrote to Jürgenson, his publisher. 'You can only buy it from the inventor, Mustel, in Paris. I want to ask you to order one of these instruments.' Keenly aware of the sensation this invention would cause in musical circles, he cautioned Jürgenson, 'Have it sent direct to Petersburg; but no-one there must know about it. I am afraid that Rimsky-Korsakov and Glazunov might hear of it and make use of the new effect before I can.'

The magical music for *The Nutcracker* was first performed at a concert of the Russian Musical Society in St Petersburg in March 1892. Tchaikovsky conducted, not the entire ballet, but the now-famous Nutcracker Suite, the only suite he ever drew from his own ballet music. Its eight sections were titled in French and listed in the order that has since become traditional: I *Ouverture miniature*. II *Danses caractéristiques*: (a) *Marche* (b) *Danse de la Fée-Dragée* (c) *Trépac, danse russe* (d) *Danse arabe* (e) *Danse chinoise* (f)

Illustration by Julius Hoffman for Kleinkinder Bilderbuch *(Little Children's Picture Book). Mechanical toys and musical instruments were very popular with German children in the late nineteenth century*

Danse des mirlitons. III *Valse des fleurs*. And the response to them was so overwhelming that nearly all were immediately repeated.

The full score, first heard at the ballet's first performance, has been called, quite simply, 'an entertainment of genius'. It is the shortest of Tchaikovsky's three ballets, but in a fleeting overture and only fifteen individual numbers it effortlessly encompasses childhood and adulthood, terror and joy, the fearful mysteries of the night and the sunny landscapes of the imagination. While always honoring Petipa's scenario, Tchaikovsky also managed to stretch its boundaries, to conjure the darker, brooding atmosphere of the Hoffmann original even as he supplied orchestrations that ideally evoked character and a ravishing bouquet of melodies that demanded dances.

Listen to the military rat-a-tat of the drums and trumpets during the fight scene, or the lush, golden brasses that establish the rich warmth of the Kingdom of Sweets at the start of Act II. For the Sugar Plum Fairy's variation, Petipa asked for 'plucked strings, 2/4, 32 bars, during which the water can be heard splashing in the fountains', and Tchaikovsky, to his eternal credit, gave him the delicate chime of the celesta, thus at the same time lyrically carving the character's personality in sound and firmly lodging the new instrument in the ranks of the orchestra.

As usual, reactions to Tchaikovsky's work were mixed. Many condemned the score as tedious, too symphonic, wrongly conceived for dancing—standard complaints—but several critics countered with unstinting praise, asserting that 'It is hard to say which number is best, for everything from beginning to end is beautiful, melodious, original and individual'. Alexandre Benois, the great designer and ballet producer who would stage his own versions of *Nutcracker* many years later, reviewed the first performance in his diary, hailing 'the music that accompanies Drosselmeyer's entrance [as], I think, the best in the ballet. It is really the work of a genius.' But he grumbled about the second act that 'at times the music reminds one of an open-air military band. Tchaikovsky has never written anything more banal than some of these numbers.'

Times change. Benois' opinion seems laughable today when the music for *The Nutcracker* is known and loved throughout the world. One of its most fervent admirers was Serge Diaghilev, who so favored the score that he appropriated a few excerpts for his own purposes. In 1911 when his Ballets Russes presented a two-act version of *Swan Lake*, Vaslav Nijinsky, as Siegfried, danced a solo to the dainty

Above
The Sugar Plum Fairy by Glyn Philpot, painted in about 1908

Sugar Plum Fairy music. Ten years later the same company offered its own adaptation of *The Sleeping Beauty* called *The Sleeping Princess*; this time the Sugar Plum Fairy's dance as well as its accompaniment appeared out of context, performed by the Lilac Fairy in the first scene. The last-act *divertissements* included a 'Persian' dance set to the leisurely *Danse arabe* and a 'Chinese' dance to the *Danse chinoise*, both choreographed by Nijinsky's sister, Bronislava Nijinska. The fabled Anna Pavlova also carried some of the music around the world with her on tour, in a ballet called *Snowflakes* by Ivan Clustine.

Tchaikovsky died just a year after the première of *The Nutcracker*, but his exquisite music, like the ballet that occasioned its birth, lives on. And if all the choreography for all the danced versions of Hoffmann's story were to disappear tomorrow, its dreamlike, fanciful events might be staged anew with only the breathtaking score as a guide.

Above
Costume design by Leon Bakst for the Mandarin in The Sleeping Princess, 1921

The Choreography

Out of more than fifty ballets that Petipa choreographed as balletmaster of the Maryinsky Theatre, *The Sleeping Beauty* is generally considered his supreme masterpiece. His second collaboration with Tchaikovsky might well have produced equally memorable results, but shortly after rehearsals began for *The Nutcracker*, Petipa fell ill and the task of choreographing the ballet fell to his assistant.

Lev Ivanov (1834–1901) was a shy, docile man, lacking both confidence and ambition, who served the Imperial Ballet for nearly fifty years, created some of the most poignant choreography of his century, and died penniless, his artistic accomplishments all but unrecognized. Having entered the *corps de ballet* of the Bolshoi Theatre in St Petersburg in 1852, he advanced more by accident than intent, finally arriving at the rank of *premier danseur* after seventeen years. He held that title until his final performance in 1893, distinguishing himself only as a mime since, as a cavalier, his nearsightedness kept him in constant fear of dropping his partner.

By the time he retired from dancing he had also proved himself too lenient to be a valuable teacher and too intimidated by responsibility to be a commanding *régisseur* or stage manager, the post to which he was promoted in 1882. Possessing, in his own words, 'too kind and weak [a] disposition' for the job, he gladly relinquished it in 1885 to become Petipa's assistant balletmaster instead. 'To be a balletmaster is not very peaceful,' he wrote, 'but still it is better than being *régisseur*.'

Ideally suited by temperament to the subservience his new post demanded, Ivanov worked in Petipa's shadow for years, patiently arranging the group dances of Petipa's ballets and devising new choreography, nearly always uncredited, for the various Maryinsky productions that failed to capture Petipa's interest. He neither sought nor received much artistic independence, but on the few occasions that chance thrust it in his path, he met the challenge resolutely, drawing invention from his exceptional musical talents.

Whatever Ivanov was not, he most definitely was a musician, gifted with absolute pitch and a phenomenal memory which together allowed him to sit down at the piano and perfectly reproduce a complicated score he had heard only once. His love of music was so great and his aptitude so marked that the director of the Theatre School (as the Maryinsky ballet school was called), where Ivanov received his training, threatened to 'let him rot for his uncontrollable inclination toward music'.

Right
Caricature of Lev Ivanov by Nicholas Legat

Below
Marius Petipa (1815–1898)

Many years later that inclination held the key to his achievements as a choreographer. In 1890, molding his taste for character dancing to Borodin's lusty music, he created Polovetsian Dances for the opera *Prince Igor* that captured all the passion and vigor of the score. And when Petipa's illness set all of *Nutcracker* before him, he responded to Tchaikovsky's genius with sensitivity and, in one number at least, with exceptional imagination.

Confined by Petipa's scenario and deprived of sufficient time to probe the score with concentrated study, as was his usual practice, Ivanov still had one opportunity to match Tchaikovsky's deeply expressive music with equally impressionistic choreography, and he took full advantage of it. Momentarily freed from the constraints of the libretto for the Dance of the Snowflakes, he focused his attention on the physical look and emotional feel of a snowstorm, and came up with a masterpiece of simplicity that embodied the music perfectly and drew unanimous praise. Sixty dancers, 'continuously interweaving', one contemporary wrote and 'dressed in white tunics with downy ornaments on their heads and snowflakes in their hands', grouped and regrouped in stars, circles, parallel and intersecting lines, as if blown by the icy wind. According to the respected teacher Agrippina Vaganova, 'connoisseurs of ballet purposely took seats in the upper tier to admire its beautiful patterns'.

The Nutcracker received its first performance on 17 December 1892 at the Maryinsky Theatre. Heading the cast were Antonietta dell'Era (an unwritten law in the Imperial Theatres decreed that the current Italian guest artist must be awarded the leading role of each new production) and the incomparable Pavel Gerdt as her cavalier, Prince Koklush.

Left
Tableau of Snowflakes from the original Maryinsky Theatre production, 1892

Riccardo Drigo conducted and the grandeur of the production grew as the evening wore on, culminating in a Waltz of the Flowers for thirty-two couples and a final scene depicting a beehive that represented civilization.

'The Nutcracker can under no condition be called a ballet,' wrote one irate critic. Another said, 'In general . . . for the dancers there was very little in the ballet, for art—absolutely nothing.' Dell'Era, whose single *pas de deux* was deemed 'wholly insignificant', was replaced almost at once by Varvara Nikitina, but casting was a minor issue. Alongside the abuse heaped on Tchaikovsky's symphonic score, Ivanov's choreography escaped relatively unscathed, but overall the ballet made so little impression that in the first three seasons of its existence, it received only fourteen performances at the Maryinsky.

Above
Dance of the Snowflakes.
New York City Ballet

Nothing remains of the original choreography but some Stepanov notation, diagrams of floor patterns written adjacent to their accompanying music. Much more of Ivanov's innovative work survives in Acts II and IV of *Swan Lake*, his second and final collaboration with Tchaikovsky and his greatest choreographic achievement. By acknowledging the pivotal place of music in ballet production and by trying to compose dance images to echo the elusive meanings of music, Ivanov helped transform the art of choreography from a decorative, often superficial exercise into a means of exploring the entire spectrum of human emotion.

When another graduate of the reknowned Theatre School decided to breathe fresh life into *The Nutcracker*, more than sixty years after its première, he unwittingly touched off an explosion of popularity for the ballet that continues unabated today. George Balanchine (1904–1983) appeared in the Maryinsky production of *Nutcracker* while he was still a student, first as a toy soldier and later as a Candy Cane in the Trepak in Act II, for which he was warmly praised, as the Mouse King and in 1919 as Prince Koklush. Only a few people at the Theatre School believed he was cut out for a career in the ballet, but those few included the great ballerina Olga Preobrajenska, who danced the Columbine doll in the first performance, and Pavel Gerdt, the original Prince Koklush, who taught Balanchine mime.

In 1954 Balanchine staged the nineteenth-century fairytale for his quintessentially twentieth-century company, the New York City Ballet. In his hands the ballet became a joyous celebration of Christmas, of childhood and of the elegant principles of classical ballet that he had learned as a boy. He restaged what he remembered of the Maryinsky production and rechoreographed the rest, handling the score with all the love and respect Ivanov had shown it and even greater knowledge, as he had much longer to study it and was a more capable musician.

Balanchine also incorporated details of plot and character from Hoffmann's original tale that had disappeared in the story's translation to the stage. Among these are a prologue showing Fritz and Clara in the hallway of their home, waiting for the party to begin and peering through the keyhole at the Christmas tree; the presence of Drosselmeyer's nephew, whom Clara first meets at the party and next encounters as the Nutcracker transformed in the Kingdom of Snow; and the nephew's explanation, in mime (quoted exactly as Balanchine had learned it in Russia, as was the Hoop Dance in the Trepak), of Clara's bravery during the battle with the mice.

Left
*Vladimir Yakovlev and two
pupils of the Maryinsky
Theatre as Mère Gigogne
(The Old Woman who
Lived in a Shoe)*

Above
*Mother Ginger and her
Polichinelles. New York
City Ballet*

*George Balanchine at work
with a member of the New
York City Ballet*

Nationally televised on Christmas Day 1958 with the choreographer himself in a rare appearance as Herr Drosselmeyer, and revised and redesigned in 1964, Balanchine's *Nutcracker* is now a cherished Christmas tradition in New York, a veteran of thirty holiday seasons. It received its 1000th New York City Ballet performance on 6 December 1983; during the winter of 1984, more than 140 companies in the United States were performing their stagings of the ballet as well. Like the Christmas tree that so amazed and delighted Clara, *The Nutcracker* continues to grow larger, brighter and more varied every year, defying its own history as if by magic.

The Revivals

Although Tchaikovsky's music, particularly the Suite, travelled quickly through Europe and to England and America, very little of the ballet was seen outside Russia until Diaghilev mounted *The Sleeping Princess* in London in 1921. In the Prologue of that production, the Lilac Fairy danced the Sugar Plum Fairy variation, thus probably introducing *The Nutcracker* to the West for the first time.

Back in St Petersburg, the ballet had languished in the Maryinsky repertory after Ivanov's death in 1901. It was revived for the first time in 1909, by Nicholas Sergeyev, the company *régisseur*, who had still been a student when the ballet had its première. During the Revolution in 1917 he mastered Stepanov notation, which the Theatre School had officially adopted in 1893, in order to teach it there without pay rather than serve in the military. The notated score Sergeyev made, along with the production notes he collected from the Maryinsky files, provided the basis for his first reconstruction of *Nutcracker* and for several important subsequent productions. Some of that material still survives; it is now considered the single most precious source for reviving Ivanov's choreography and our only link to it.

When *The Nutcracker* first appeared in Moscow, in 1919, it was staged at the Bolshoi Theatre by the *régisseur*, Alexander Gorsky. Though a former pupil of Petipa's, Gorsky was more interested in making ballet expressive than in its formal design. In his *Nutcracker*, he stuck firmly to the narrative in Act I, depicting a characteristic nineteenth-century German household in realistic detail. But in Act II, little Masha (as Clara is called in Russian productions) was suddenly transformed into a ballerina, who claimed the Sugar Plum Fairy music for her own and shared the *grand pas de deux* with the Nutcracker, now also transformed into a prince. By banishing the Sugar Plum Fairy and her cavalier and by replacing children with adults, Gorsky inaugurated a lasting tradition.

Feodor Lopukhov had even more innovative ideas about choreography. Balletmaster of the Maryinsky throughout the 1920s, he managed not only to preserve the classical repertory through the arduous days of the Revolution but to experiment with it as well. In his deliberately controversial *Nutcracker* of 1928, he divided the action into twenty-two episodes, gave the dancers a text to speak, from Hoffmann's story, and acrobatic steps to perform, and also used them as stagehands to move the constructivist-inspired panels that made up the set. At one point, the Sugar Plum Fairy was carried onstage upside down with her legs spread in a split.

Above
The adults at the Christmas party. Royal Ballet, 1984

Below

Pacific North West Ballet, 1984

That production caused a great uproar and was rapidly and officially discredited. But the next *Nutcracker* at the Kirov, staged in 1934 by Vassily Vainonen, became the foundation for all Soviet productions to come. Vainonen returned to the traditional flavor of the original and to traditionally classical choreography. More importantly, he expanded both Masha's role and the psychological aspects of the story, using Masha's love for the Nutcracker as a link between the realistic first scene—the only one in which she appeared as a child—and the fantastic incidents that followed. Having introduced a romance between Masha and the Nutcracker when he rescues her from the mice, Vainonen let the *grand pas de deux* represent the culmination and fulfilment of their love.

Above
*The Battle of the Mice.
Royal Ballet, 1984*

This production is still danced by the Kirov Ballet today, more than fifty years after its creation. Following its enormous success in Leningrad, it replaced Gorsky's version in Moscow, where it was danced until 1966 when the present director of the Bolshoi Ballet, Yuri Grigorovich, replaced it with his own, which harked back to Gorsky in using an adult Masha but went a step further. It made Masha the only 'real' character in the ballet and set the entire tale in her imagination, where her thoughts alone endow the kindly Toy Maker and the Nutcracker Prince with life. Grigorovich decided that a single ballerina should dance the triple role of Masha, the Snow Queen and the Sugar Plum Fairy, since he felt the latter two characters are merely guises in which Masha imagines herself. Conceived as a marvelous dream peopled with dancing candles and Christmas trees, the production has enormous sweetness

and innocence. It ends, logically, with Masha awakening at home and finding the toy nutcracker nestled in her lap.

Thanks to Sergeyev's notes and notation, *The Nutcracker* had a longer and more varied life than anyone, especially Ivanov, might have predicted. Its first complete performance outside Russia took place in England in 1934, just three years after Ninette de Valois founded the Vic-Wells (now Royal) Ballet. Although the troupe initially consisted of only six full-time dancers and de Valois, her declared intention was to build a great English company, using the nineteenth-century classics as the foundation of the repertory and of the young dancers' training. Accordingly, she invited Nicholas Sergeyev to stage these works for her.

The cast for *The Nutcracker*, or *Casse-Noisette* as it was then called, was massive for the tiny stage at the Sadler's Wells Theatre; it included forty dancers, a group of children

Above

Margot Fonteyn and Robert Helpmann as the Sugar Plum Fairy and her cavalier. Vic-Wells Ballet, 1937

from the Lord Mayor's Boys Players, and the actress Elsa Lanchester, whose movements as Ariel in a rehearsal of *The Tempest* convinced Sergeyev that she should perform the *Danse arabe*. Sergeyev was guided by the Stepanov notation, which he had brought with him when he left Russia after the October Revolution of 1917, and assisted by Lydia Lopokova, who had danced Aurora and the Lilac Fairy for Diaghilev in 1921 and appeared as the Vic-Wells' first Swanilda in *Coppélia* in 1933. Frederick Ashton recalls that 'Lydia rehearsed the young dancer taking the part of Clara—a part which she had danced before the Tsar during her school days at the Imperial Ballet School in St Petersburg at the age of nine. She had never danced in, nor seen, the ballet again until the Sadler's Wells revival, but she could still remember the steps.'

On opening night, 30 January 1934, de Valois' long-cherished dream of establishing a world-class classical company moved one step closer to reality. Alicia Markova, often called the first English ballerina (she was born Alice Marks), graced the first night and the entire production with her exquisite performance of the Sugar Plum Fairy. Four months later, a dark-eyed dancer, only fourteen years old, slipped into the *corps de ballet* as a last-minute substitute and made her professional debut as a Snowflake. When the company staged the ballet again in 1937, the teenager danced the delicate ballerina role; by then, and ever after, she was known as Margot Fonteyn.

Copy of a design by Alexandre Benois for Act I décor. London Festival Ballet, 1957

On 24 October 1950, at the Stoll Theatre in London, another English ballet company came to life. Nicholas Beriozoff staged a new, very traditional *Nutcracker* to mark the occasion, and Alicia Markova, this time with her favorite partner, Anton Dolin, led the young, hopeful dancers in an auspicious first night. Despite the modesty of a production with neither children nor fantastic stage effects, this first *Nutcracker* brought the fledgeling Festival Ballet its first success and the nucleus of a faithful audience.

The next time that company mounted *The Nutcracker*, it enlisted the combined talents of dancer-choreographer David Lichine and producer-designer Alexandre Benois. Benois, who had attended the ballet's première in 1892, had already staged it once; working with the ballet company of La Scala, Milan in 1938, he had tried to improve on the dramatic coherence of the original libretto. To link the first and second acts smoothly, he joined the Christmas party to the snow scene without any pause or interruption, and just as the Stahlbaum drawing room dissolved into the enchanted, snowy forest, little Clara became a grown-up ballerina and the little nutcracker a grown-up prince.

In the new production, he strengthened Clara's role even further, discarding the Snow Queen—an innovation from the 1950 production—so Clara could dance with the Nutcracker Prince in the snow scene, and assigning her a lively dance in the prologue and all the explanatory mime in the Kingdom of Sweets. Bringing Drosselmeyer into that last scene, as the ruler of the Kingdom, provided another link to unify the action. And since Benois was determined that not a single note of the score be wasted, Lichine choreographed a new prologue, outside the drawing room, and a *divertissement* for Madame Régnier, the *bonbonnière*, and her brood of little Polichinelles (both of which Balanchine had restored in his 1954 version).

The production opened at the Royal Festival Hall on 24 December 1957 with Natalie Krassovska and John Gilpin as the principals and Anton Dolin as a cheerfully eccentric Drosselmeyer. The press and public loved it, and it was danced every Christmas season for almost twenty years. Ronald Hynd's version, which succeeded it in 1976 and is still performed now, focused on the story as Hoffmann told it, contrasting the bourgeois German household, complete down to Frau Stahlbaum's social pretensions, with the fanciful delights of Clara's dreams. Actually, Clara and her older sister Louise, a character Hoffmann invented, dream the magical second act together. In it, Clara remains a

Drawing of Herr Drosselmeyer which probably inspired the designs for the Royal Ballet production in 1984, from the Annals of the Imperial Russian Theatres, *1892*

child, indulged by the doting Drosselmeyer with a luscious entertainment, while Louise explores a more mature fantasy in her romantic *pas de deux* with Drosselmeyer's nephew, Karl.

In a program note for the most recent Royal Ballet revival, which opened at the Royal Opera House on 20 December 1984, the producer, Peter Wright, supplied the audience with an explanation of the story they were about to see rather than a synopsis. This background information, direct from Hoffmann's tale, could not easily be put on the stage, but it described the relationship of the characters and the motives for their actions. Wright also carried out an extensive search for the ballet's authentic choreography. Leaning heavily on Sergeyev's notes and Stepanov nota-tion, now in the Harvard Theatre Collection, and on the memories of dancers like Markova, he staged either Ser-geyev's renderings or his own of the Ivanov choreography for the Dolls' dances, *Grossvater* dance and Snowflakes in Act I and the *Danse des Mirlitons* and *Valse des Fleurs* in Act II. The *grand pas de deux* was credited to Ivanov alone.

Wright stated that 'the story is about Drosselmeyer'. In another noteworthy Royal Ballet revival, Clara dominated the story instead; one saw it through her eyes and felt it with her feelings. Rudolf Nureyev's version, first staged for the Royal Swedish Ballet in 1967 with sumptuous designs by Nicholas Georgiadis, entered the repertory of the Royal Ballet on 29 February 1968, with Merle Park as Clara and Nureyev as both Drosselmeyer and the Nutcracker Prince. There were no children in the production, no Sugar Plum Fairy and no Kingdom of Sweets. Clara remained herself throughout, a girl about to become a woman, and all her adventures sprang from her imagination. Falling asleep as the Christmas party drew to a close, she dreamed of the battle with the mice and the nutcracker transformed into a prince. Then she saw her family and their friends trans-formed into terrifying bats, who attacked her in a mysteri-ous grotto. Finally she found herself inside her own toy theatre, dancing happily with all her dolls and then ecstatically with her handsome prince. The dream and the Christmas party ended together as she awoke.

When Mikhail Baryshnikov staged his version of The *Nutcracker* for American Ballet Theatre in 1976, he added a further psychological twist. Clara was still the heroine, the Nutcracker Prince still a dream figure conjured by Drossel-meyer, who was still Clara's godfather in the real world. But as Clara dreams, she discovers that maturity can bring disappointment with it as well as happiness.

Herr Drosselmeyer and Clara watch the magical Christmas tree grow into a tower of lights. Royal Ballet, 1984

Because she has acted bravely and saved the nutcracker from the mice, Drosselmeyer grants her a dream of love, which is her voyage with the prince to his beautiful kingdom where she dances with him and with his subjects. At the peak of her happiness the dream starts to fade; everything in the court disappears. The passionate *pas de deux* becomes a poignant *pas de trois*, with Drosselmeyer both supporting Clara as she expresses her love ('lending moral support,' wrote one critic, as she 'isn't quite old enough to live happily ever after'), and drawing her away from her romantic dream and back to reality.

Both Nureyev and Baryshnikov were members of the Kirov Ballet before their respective defections to the West, and each of them preserves an extract from the Vainonen production in his own: in Nureyev's, it is the prince's variation in Act II and in Baryshnikov's, the Snowflake waltz. Neither production is particularly light-hearted; neither features children or tinsel or the kind of fairyland fantasy that is the essence of most stagings; but both have proved enormously popular. Baryshnikov's version has been filmed for television and is regularly broadcast at Christmas, and Nureyev's is currently danced in Paris.

But if you say *Nutcracker* to most people in America, they will think of Balanchine's festive, sugar-dusted spectacle, or of one of its innumerable glittering offshoots. They will also think of children, the hushed, wide-eyed children who see the ballet by the thousands every year, and the hundreds more, even more lucky perhaps, who appear in it as mice, soldiers, angels, enchanted toys and animals of every description.

The first time *Nutcracker* was danced in America, however, it was given by adults for adults. Alicia Markova led the cast, with the noble André Eglevsky as her partner, in the Ballet Russe de Monte Carlo production, which opened on 17 October 1940 at the 51st Street Theatre in New York, in a shortened staging by Alexandra Fedorova. It quickly became a staple of the company's repertory for its hectic tours, and often shared a program with Balanchine's *Serenade* and Leonide Massine's *Capriccio Espagnol*.

A former vaudevillian and ballet dancer named Willam Christensen mounted the first complete American *Nutcracker* on the San Francisco Ballet in 1944. He cast Gisella Caccialanza as the Sugar Plum Fairy and skillfully shaped the choreography to the quick, brilliant technique she had learned from her godfather, Enrico Cecchetti, a noted dancer and mime in his own right and one of the most important teachers of this century. Leaving his brother Lew

Above
The Nutcracker Prince leaps into battle. American Ballet Theatre

Below
The children at the Christmas party. Bolshoi Ballet

in charge of the company and the production, Willam then returned to his native Utah, where he developed a company at the University of Utah and set *The Nutcracker* on that small group in 1955. Ballet West still makes its home in Salt Lake City and still performs Will Christensen's *Nutcracker* annually.

Country by country and production by production, *The Nutcracker* has grown to its present amazing proportions. An English dancer, Celia Franca, brought it to Canada in 1951; a South African, John Cranko, choreographed it in Stuttgart in 1966; and an American, John Neumeier, created a version in Frankfurt in 1969 that discarded much of the original libretto and turned *The Nutcracker* into a ballet about ballet. Nourished by the national customs and colors it has absorbed, *The Nutcracker* now seems indestructible, a fabulous creature that speaks of magic and dreams in all languages.

The Designs

Although Vsevolojsky sketched out his own ideas for the costumes of the original 1892 production, the design credit was officially shared by K.M. Ivanov, who did Act I, and Mikhail Botcharov, a company designer with a particular flair for exterior scenes, who did Act II. In his diary the day after the opening, Benois described their work in scathing terms:

The décor of Scene 1 ... is both disgusting and profoundly shocking ... Instead of having an elaborate chamber in Rococo or Louis XVI style, lit by chandeliers and sconces, but conveying at the same time an atmosphere of good-natured bourgeoisie, we are obliged to contemplate ... the salon of some rich parvenu banker ... It was stupid, coarse, heavy and dark ... The costumes, too, are stupidly chosen ... The second act is still worse ... The costumes are elaborate but lacking in taste; some of the dancers are in bright yellow, others in bright pink and the effect can only be called 'loud'.

Years later, in his *Reminiscences*, Benois allowed that 'the only setting of artistic merit was Botcharov's moon-lit and snow-covered forest', and contemporary photographs reveal the costumes for that scene, dotted with powder

Above
Design for the Nutcracker by Alexandre Benois for London Festival Ballet, 1957

Below
Design for a doll's house and two dolls by Benois

puffs of snow on the skirts, bodices and over the shoulder. The short wands, stuck with light snowballs, that Balanchine's Snowflakes carry today are direct descendants of the original designs; however, the sunbursts of snowpuffs that Ivanov's *corps de ballet* wore as head-dresses have long since vanished.

As Benois pointed out in his *Memoirs*, he was 'avid for anything exotic or eerie and terrifying in my childhood, and even in later years. My fondness for E. Th. A. Hoffmann, whom I came across when I was fifteen, was due to this inclination.' His own productions reflected these passions, as well as his love for 'the charm of the miniature toy world'. What a lovely miniature he created at the end of his snow scene at La Scala in 1938: having danced their first 'adult' *pas de deux*, Clara and her Nutcracker Prince wrapped themselves snugly in white fur coats and drove away in a sleigh drawn by white polar bears.

The present Scottish Ballet production, choreographed by Peter Darrell with designs by Philip Prowse, also boasts a pair of polar bears, who are escorts to the Snow Queen, and Kent Stowell has choreographed *divertissements* for an alluring peacock and a huge Chinese tiger in his Seattle

Below
The Sugar Plum Fairy enters the Kingdom of Sweets.
National Ballet of Canada

production. But the mystery and enchantment of most productions derive less from the presence of extraordinary animals, very few of whom inhabit Hoffmann's vivid story, than from extraordinary events.

In Hoffmann's original, Clara left her cosy home on her own two feet, walking into a 'delightfully-scented meadow, from which rose millions of sparks like gleaming gems' through the sleeve of her father's coat. For her travels in the ballet, through the snowy forest and on to this marvelous wonderland, Benois placed her inside a huge, self-propelling walnut; for Peter Wright's production, Julia Trevelyan Oman created an airy sleigh, piloted across the stage by a gilded angel framed in an arc of lights. Balanchine's Clara rides in her own brass bed, sleeping peacefully as it glides silently through the snow.

At the start of Grigorovich's dream sequence in the Bolshoi production, Masha and her Prince step into a toy boat that swings them up off the ground toward the top of the Christmas tree. As they swing up, the Toymaker drops out of the sky to meet them, floating downward under a big, black umbrella. And the Sugar Plum Fairy in Celia Franca's 1964 production for the National Ballet of Canada also appeared out of the sky; for her entrance into the Kingdom of Sweets, Jürgen Rose designed a dainty filigree basket, buoyed by a dozen bright balloons.

Fairies, of course, can float even without balloons, as a famous photograph of an early *Nutcracker* performance clearly demonstrates. Peter Wright has taken pains to duplicate this charming effect, briefly perching his ballerina *en arabesque* on a filmy silver fabric, as has Balanchine, whose Sugar Plum Fairy skims across the stage in the same *arabesque* position, supported only by her partner's outstretched hand.

The best-loved of these miraculous stage effects is undoubtedly the growth of the Christmas tree, which

Engraving from the Annals *of the Imperial Russian Theatres, 1893*

Hoffmann didn't mention at all and Petipa described only by saying, 'The fir tree seemed to grow enormous.' According to Balanchine, who used Horace Armistead's designs in 1954, the tree was the most important part of the production: 'It's a tree of plenty. It represents food, plenty, life ... Baum [managing director of City Center in 1954] gave me $40,000. We studied how the tree could grow both up and also out, like an umbrella. The tree cost $25,000 and Baum was angry. "George," he said, "can't you do it without the tree?" I said, "[The ballet] *is* the tree."'

But not every company could realize such spectacular visions, and the difficulties posed by necessity frequently yielded delightful solutions. When Gorsky's production opened in 1919, tarlatan for the Snowflakes' tutus was completely unobtainable, so the designer, Constantin Korovine, dressed them instead in copies of Russian fur coats and put muffs on their hands. And since Frederick Ashton produced his one-act version of *Casse Noisette* (1951) for the Sadler's Wells Theatre Ballet, which was perpetually on tour, Cecil Beaton had to devise designs that would be practical as well as evocative. His setting for the

Varvara Nikitina and Pavel Gerdt as the Sugar Plum Fairy and Prince Koklush in the original Maryinsky production, 1892

Kingdom of Snow was only a backcloth, a scribble of trees outlined in black on a pale ground, which could be folded, transported and rehung with ease. The costumes, however, were richly ornamented and frosted with spangles; the Snow Queen wore a pearly white wig, a crown of icicles and a tutu trimmed with ermine tails.

Design by Mstislav Doboujinsky for the décor of the Snow scene. Vic-Wells Ballet, 1937

The companies that choose to powder the stage with snow as the Snowflakes dance face a different problem, since the dancers' safety must always take precedence over the ultimate effect. Once the floor becomes slippery, dancing becomes dangerous, and so at various times confetti, shredded plastic film and even cloth have been used to create the proper illusion. Before the opening night of Lichine's 1957 production, members of the Festival Ballet Club patiently cut strips of nylon into 750,000 tiny pieces of snow.

Perhaps nothing has given designers as much pleasure as creating the delectable fairy-tale atmosphere of the Kingdom of Sweets. James Bailey, who designed Alfred Rodrigues' 1956 revival at La Scala, took his inspiration from the breathtaking work of Carl Fabergé, court jeweller to Tsar Nicholas II. David Walker gave the Louisville Ballet a pink and gold Victorian valentine for its last act, while Rouben

Ter-Arutunian turned the backdrop for Balanchine's 1964 version into a mouthwatering extravaganza of meringue, marzipan, gumdrops and chocolate.

In 1983, having already written and illustrated many children's books, Maurice Sendak ventured into ballet for the first time at the behest of Kent Stowell, director of the Pacific Northwest Ballet in Seattle. For Stowell's ambitious new *Nutcracker*, Sendak designed seven settings and 180 costumes, mingling reality and fantasy with fluent ease: thus the magical Eastern seraglio that Clara discovers in her dream-world derives from the Chinese wallpaper and Oriental statues that decorate her parents' comfortable home.

Infinitely seductive, *The Nutcracker* stretches invitingly before an artist like a blank canvas. It has been draped with curtains of sugar drops, framed in Moorish arches, bordered with lacy paper cut-outs, brushed with streaks of gold. Adapting their skills and plumbing their imaginations to satisfy its demands, designers through the years have found a whole variety of bold and glorious images to enhance every production.

Clara and Fritz in the Kingdom of Sweets. Cleveland Ballet

The Nutcracker Industry

In the end, every interpretation of *The Nutcracker* mingles fantasy with reality since, whatever form it might assume, the work is created for pleasure but sold for money. Especially in recent years, *The Nutcracker* has developed into a thriving industry, the golden goose in the box office of many ballet companies that annually lays golden eggs amounting to one-third or more of those companies' annual revenue. Astonishing figures were published in December 1984, outlining the extent to which some companies can rely on their holiday money-maker. In the fiscal year prior to that publication date, the New York City Ballet, for example, operated on a budget of $17 million; the company gave thirty-eight performances of *The Nutcracker* which earned $1,869,000, twenty-three per cent of the total ticket income for the year. Pacific Northwest Ballet had an operating budget for the same year of $3.7 million; twenty-six performances of the glowing Stowell-Sendak production earned $1,444,648, a whopping sixty per cent of the year's total from ticket sales.

Walt Disney's seductive white fish which perform the Arabian dance in Fantasia

Both these companies and many others around the world are selling children dreams along with the dancing. While the ballet stays forever on the stage, out of reach and unattainable once the curtain has fallen, little carved nutcrackers can be carried home to bed. Dolls, stuffed animals, emblazoned T-shirts, sweatshirts and towels, and records of the music fill the boutique shelves in the theatres—but not for long—and many of these items can be purchased as gifts from dance shops or department stores.

In fact, *The Nutcracker*'s popularity has become so great that its name and characters can be marketed without the ballet. An artist in Texas advertises his 'art print', which depicts a still-life arrangement of a leather-framed picture of a dancer, a pair of satin pointe shoes and a small carved nutcracker on a rocking horse. An Illinois manufacturer offers a Sugar Plum Fairy 'bone china figurine ... individually sculpted' and a pair of pink porcelain pointe shoes standing on a music box that plays the Waltz of the Flowers. There are recipes for *Casse-Noisette Chicken* and *Sugarplum Flan*, and stores in Toronto and Johannesburg named The Nutcracker Sweet.

Ivanov probably bears less responsibility for the infectious spread of *The Nutcracker* than does Tchaikovsky, whose Nutcracker Suite, as Balanchine shrewdly pointed out, has been 'a million-dollar title in America' for years. And perhaps the largest share of the credit for popularizing the music belongs to Walt Disney, whose animated movie *Fantasia* (1940) contains one of its most picturesque visual

The inscrutable mushrooms, performers of the Chinese dance

interpretations. According to a Disney biography, in selecting the Nutcracker Suite for this film Disney 'wasn't aiming at anything highbrow. Nor was he trying to bring classical music to the mass audiences. He was simply trying to use serious music as another tool for animation.'

His large, inventive staff of artists created memorable likenesses for each musical selection without resorting to a single human face or form. The Chinese dance fell to six inscrutable mushrooms, the Trepak to a prickly handful of Scotch thistles, and the Arabian dance to a seductive white fish, provocatively shrouded in her own diaphanous fins and tail. The artist who drew the Sugar Plum Fairies had hummingbirds in mind, along with Disney's admonition to the entire staff that the fifteen-minute sequence of six dances 'should be something beautiful and something fantastic . . . It's the fairyland thing we are picturing.'

Disney's film was only the beginning. As productions multiplied and even fairyland became familiar, choreographers began to reconceive the entire work. They invented

Original drawings for the thistles which dance the Trepak

not only new characters, but locations, situations and motivations to suit the size of their companies and budgets and the public's fancy. Who knows how many alterations now flourish in ballets across America bearing titles like *Nutcracker Fantasy*, *The Magic Nutcracker*, *Alternutcracker* and *Winter Carnival and other Sugar Plums*? There is *A Jazz Nutcracker* in Pittsburgh and a *Jazz Nutcracker Fantasie* in San Diego, and at Ballet West in Salt Lake City, the updating of Willam Christensen's production has bestowed the face of the film character E.T. on Mother Ginger.

Dorothy Hamill and Robin Cousins, both winners of Olympic gold medals for figure skating, joined forces to present *Nutcracker: A Fantasy on Ice*, an elaborate display of sequins and icy pyrotechnics. Darrell Hildebrandt, program coordinator for a public library in Bismarck, North Dakota, had read a book about *The Nutcracker* but never actually seen it when he created his own unique staging for eighty life-sized puppets. Moving through the story like actors, with Tchaikovsky's score as accompaniment, each puppet was maneuvered by two humans, swathed in black from head to toe in the manner of Japanese stagehands to render their bodies and their manipulations theatrically 'invisible'.

In 1982, a modern dance choreographer named Tandy Beal unveiled an equally remarkable production in Santa Cruz, California, after deciding to stick with the traditional plot but to abandon traditional dancing, both ballet *and* modern. More an exuberant holiday entertainment than any kind of formal dance production, hers is probably the only *Nutcracker* on earth in which jugglers, flamenco dancers, roller skaters and gymnasts proudly and joyously parade their skills through the Act II *divertissements*.

Every year, *The Nutcracker* reappears in opera houses, municipal theatres and elementary school auditoriums. Refreshed and revitalized after its long summer slumber, its innocence seems ever more welcome, its form more splendid, its spirit more hopeful and jubilant. It makes adults dream of childhood and children dream of magic, and this, as the critic Edwin Denby wrote of the last scene, 'leads to a happy dazzle for everything and everybody everywhere at once'.

The Kingdom of Sweets in Tandy Beal's imaginative staging

Index

Acknowledgments
American Ballet Theatre/Martha Swope 36−7;
Atlanta Ballet/Kenneth T Hertz 14−5;
Tandy Beal 47;
Bethnal Green Museum 19;
Cleveland Ballet 43;
© Walt Disney Productions 45−6;
Dominic Photography 27, 30−1, 35;
London Festival Ballet 32;
Novosti 24, 26;
Pacific North West Ballet/Don Cooper 28;
Private collection 20−1;
Royal Ballet Benevolent Fund 6, 42;
Royal Ballet School 21;
Royal College of Music 17;
Society for Cultural Relations with the USSR 36;
Martha Swope 25, 26−7;
Theatre Museum/Gordon Anthony 31;
Victoria and Albert Museum 38, 29;
Reg Wilson 28−9.